PYTHON MULTIPLE CHOICE

Python is one of the most loved programming languages, enabling you to do complex tasks while being easy to learn with a clear syntax. Over the last few years, more and more people have started to learn how to code in Python, not just developers, data scientists and software engineers.

You've been studying Python for a while now or you've just started and somehow wonder where you stand with your knowledge of this awesome programming language?

Test your Python skills with this multiple choice quiz and see for yourself. Feel free to use this book as an indication for where you stand on certain Python subjects. Taking this multiple choice test will let you know which topics you should revise and which ones you already have a good knowledge of.

While taking the multiple choice test, remember: For each question, only one answer is right. The right answers can be found in the answers section starting on page 36.

Enjoy!

CONTENT

QUESTIONS

BASIC PYTHON

PRINTING

Q: What does the print() function do?
- ☐ It tells the printer to print any open document using the default printer.
- ☐ It helps to debug printing errors.
- ☐ It allows to look for bugs in the code by printing bugfree parts.
- ☐ It displays things to the console.

Q: Which of these command lines will print "Hello World"?
- ☐ say("Hello World!")
- ☐ print()("Hello World!")
- ☐ output:(("Hello World!"))
- ☐ print("Hello World!")

Q: What's the command print() in Python?
- ☐ A function
- ☐ A list
- ☐ A variable
- ☐ An array

Q: Which of the following examples for the print() function *does not* lead to an error output?
- ☐ print(5)
- ☐ print(„foo")
- ☐ print(True)
- ☐ print:self

Q: What is the output of multiple print() functions? E.g. these:
print ("I love my ")
print ("dog!")
- ☐ "I love my dog!"
- ☐ Python doesn't work with multiple print() functions, it will output an error.
- ☐ I love my
  dog!
- ☐ It will print only "I love my " and stop there.

STRINGS

Q: Which one of these is a string?
- ☐ "you"
- ☐ <are>
- ☐ *so*
- ☐ ;right;

Q: How can you add whitespaces in between combined strings?
- ☐ print ("That's" + whitespace + "true!")
- ☐ print ("That's" + " " + "true!")
- ☐ print ("That's" + < > + "true!")
- ☐ print ("That's" + __ + "true!")

Q: Sometimes, you want to know the number of characters in a string. What's the name of the function that will return the length of a string?
- ☐ num()
- ☐ length()
- ☐ len()
- ☐ count()

Q: What is the output of this code:
print(len("Hello world!"))
- ☐ syntax error due to double brackets.
- ☐ 10, as whitepsaces and special characters are not counted.
- ☐ 12, as all characters within the quotation marks are counted.
- ☐ 14, as all characters within the brackets are counted.

Q: Let's look at added lengths of strings: What is the output of this code:
print(len("Nice") + len("job!"))
- ☐ 8
- ☐ 7
- ☐ 6
- ☐ 5

Q: How can you identify a string?
- ☐ They are always surrounded by brackets.
- ☐ They are always inside of functions.
- ☐ They are always surrounded by single or double quotation marks.
- ☐ They are always written in italic.

Q: How can you display a string to the console?
- ☐ This is not possible.
- ☐ Use the function len().
- ☐ Write strings in italic.
- ☐ Use the function print().

Q: What is the output of this code?
print(len("Well") + ("done!"))
- ☐ 7
- ☐ 8
- ☐ 9
- ☐ 10

VARIABLES

Q: What are variables in Python?
- ☐ Variables are a set of attributes.
- ☐ Variables are symbols that represents a quantity.
- ☐ Variables store values in a name so that the name can later be used to refer to the value.
- ☐ Variables are a way to display things to the console.

Q: What is the output of this code?
animal = "dormouse"
print(animal)
- ☐ animal
- ☐ dormouse
- ☐ error: invalid syntax
- ☐ print

Q: Combining different variables, what is the output of this code?
cat = "tom"
mouse = "jerry"
print(cat + mouse)
- ☐ tomjerry
- ☐ tom+jerry
- ☐ tom jerry
- ☐ jerrytom

Q: What happens in this case?
print(animal)
animal = "fox"
- ☐ Python prints fox to the console, as animal = fox.
- ☐ Python prints animal to the console, as this is the first command line.
- ☐ Python prints nothing.
- ☐ Python prints an error message saying the name "animal" is not defined.

Q: Variables can be updated by setting them to a new value. What is the output of the following code?

animal = "Shellfish"
animal = "Octopus"
print(animal)

- ☐ Octopus
- ☐ Nothing
- ☐ Shellfish
- ☐ animal

Q: When naming the variables, use a descriptive name and avoid using operators. What are invalid variable names?

- ☐ =
- ☐ *
- ☐ +
- ☐ animal

Q: What is the main benefit of using variables?

- ☐ Variables use the same value in many places.
- ☐ Variables use many values in the same place.
- ☐ Variables store many values in a single name.
- ☐ Variables set many names to the same value.

NUMBERS

Q: What are the different types of numbers in Python?

- ☐ Integers
- ☐ Strings
- ☐ Floats
- ☐ Signs

Q: What are integers?

- ☐ Numbers with a decimal point like 1.125.
- ☐ Whole numbers like 2, 6 or -80.
- ☐ Special characters like ?, ! or #.
- ☐ Numbers in percent, like 75%.

Q: Sometimes, it is helpful to convert a string to a number. What function does this?

- ☐ num()
- ☐ str()
- ☐ int()
- ☐ con()

Q: What is printed to the console?

```
y = int("2")
print(y)
```

☐   2
☐   "2"
☐   y
☐   "y"

Q: What is the output of this code?

```
int("Hello world!")
```

☐   "Hello world"
☐   ValueError: invalid literal for int()
☐   12
☐   SyntaxError: invalid syntax

Q: Converting a string to a number, what does Python print to the console?

```
text = "12"
print(int(text))
```

☐   The number 12
☐   The string "12"
☐   The string "text"
☐   ValueError: invalid literal for int()

Q: Using numbers in Python, it is possible to calculate with them? What is the output of this code?

```
x = 2
y = 4
z = x + y
print(z)
```

☐   2
☐   4
☐   6
☐   8

Q: So we can add numbers in Python. What else can we calculate?
☐   multiply values using *
☐   subtract values using -
☐   divide values using /
☐   we can calculate nothing else

Q: What is the output of this code?

```
x = 60
y = 2
z = (x + y)/y
print(z)
```

☐ 21
☐ 31
☐ 41
☐ 51

Q: What is the output of this code?

```
zodiac = 100
sign = 4
print((zodiac*sign)+(zodiac/sign))
```

☐ 425
☐ 4
☐ 104
☐ 208

BOOLEANS

Q: A boolean is a value which can be:
☐ Right
☐ True
☐ Wrong
☐ False

Q: What are the values True and False equivalent to in Python?
☐ 0 and 1
☐ 1 and 0
☐ 2 and 1
☐ 1 and 2

Q: If True equals 1 and False equals 0, what is the output of this code?

```
light = False
darkness = 0
print(light == 0)
```

☐ False
☐ True
☐ 0
☐ light

Q: What does Python print to the console?

code = False

print(int(code))

- ☐ 0
- ☐ 1
- ☐ 2
- ☐ 3

Q: What does Python print to the console?

code = False

print(bool(code))

- ☐ 0
- ☐ False
- ☐ True
- ☐ 1

Q: What are the different boolean operators?

- ☐ and
- ☐ so
- ☐ or
- ☐ not

Q: Boolean values can be combined using and 'and' operator. True and True equals True. What equals True and False?

- ☐ Also True.
- ☐ Error message due to contradicting booleans.
- ☐ False.
- ☐ Nothing is printed to the console because it can't be compiled.

Q: What is the output when using the 'or' operator in this case: True or False?

- ☐ True.
- ☐ True and False.
- ☐ False.
- ☐ Nothing is printed to the console because it can't be compiled.

Q: Using the operator 'not' to negate a boolean value, what is the result of 'not False'?

- ☐ True.
- ☐ Not False.
- ☐ False.
- ☐ Nothing is printed to the console because it can't be compiled.

Q: Making a boolean value the opposite of whatever it currently is, what is the output of the following code?

warm = True
cold = not warm
print(cold)

☐ cold
☐ cot warm
☐ False
☐ True

Q: Put your boolean operators to the test: what is the single boolean value of e?

c = True
d = False
e = (c or d) and (c and d)

☐ False
☐ True
☐ True and False
☐ False and True

IF STATEMENTS

Q: What do if statements do?
- ☐ They allow a Python program to choose from multiple options.
- ☐ They allow a Python program to compile the code.
- ☐ They allow a Python program to make decisions based on boolean expressions.
- ☐ They allow a Python program to infer values from variables.

Q: What would Python print to the console according to the following code?

warm = True
if warm == False:
  print("It's cold.")

- ☐ It's cold.
- ☐ warm
- ☐ False
- ☐ Nothing is printed to the console, since warm is not equal to False.

Q: How does the if statement exactly work?
- ☐ The code following the keyword 'if' has to be a boolean expression. If the expression evaluates to be True, then the code in the if statement will be executed.
- ☐ The code has to contain the 'if' keyword but doesn't need to be True to be executed.
- ☐ The expression needs to equal to True, but also works without the 'if' keyword.
- ☐ The boolean expression needs to equal to False or otherwise the if statement won't work.

Q: Applying multiple if statements, what does Python print to the console?

height = 20
if height >= 10:
  print("medium")
if height >= 20:
  print("tall")

- ☐ It will print only "medium".
- ☐ It will print only "tall".
- ☐ It will print the height, so "20".
- ☐ It will print both words, since both if statements are met:
  medium
  tall

Q: Combining different conditions, what does Python print to the console?

temp = 8
cold = 0
sunshine = False
rain = True
if rain == sunshine or (temp < cold):
   print("No thank you.")
if temp > cold:
   print("Alright.")

☐ It will print "Alright.", since rain doesn't equal sunshine and temp isn't less than cold.
☐ It will print "No thank you.", since the operator used is 'or'.
☐ Syntax error: There can't be both a False and a True value defined before an if statement.
☐ It will print print nothing to the console, since neither one of the conditions is true.

ELSE IF AND ELSE

Q: Why does it make sense to use an else if statement?
☐ Instead of using multiple if statements, it can be used chaining multiple conditions together.
☐ It allows for a second, third or fourth if statement after having used a first one.
☐ It only makes sense to use an else if statement if there is anything else to write.
☐ Multiple if statements testing different conditions are always better than else if statements.

Q: What is the keyword used for writing an else if statement?
☐ elseif
☐ ifel
☐ elif
☐ else-if

Q: What is the output of this code?

```
warm = 20

if warm > 30:
  print("very warm")
if warm > 20:
  print("warm")
if warm > 10:
  print("pleasant")
```

- ☐ 10
- ☐ warm
- ☐ pleasant
- ☐ 20

Q: In a code where the first if condition is True, what happens to the other else if condition?
- ☐ It will be checked regardless of the first condition.
- ☐ It will be ignored since the first condition is True.
- ☐ It will be checked against the first condition.
- ☐ The first condition needs to be False so that the second condition gets checked.

Q: What is the output of this code?

```
length = 1
if length > 10:
  print("longest")
if length > 1:
  print("long")
if length < 1 :
  print("short")
```

- ☐ It will print nothing to the console, since < and > means that the value needs to be either smaller or greater.
- ☐ long
- ☐ short
- ☐ shortest

Q: What is true of the else if condition?
- ☐ You cannot start with an else if statement, it needs to come after an if statement.
- ☐ You can start with an else if statement.
- ☐ More than one else if statement will lead to an error.
- ☐ More than five else if statements will lead to a runtime error.

Q: You can add an else condition to the end of an if block. What does this mean for the execution of the if statements?

☐ The code in the else block will be executed only if the condition in the if statement before it is true.

☐ If the condition in the if statement before the else condition is false, the code in the else block will be executed.x

☐ Both the if statement and the else statement will be executed.

☐ If you add an else statement, the if statement before that will be ignored.

Q: What is the output of the following code?

grade = 40
if grade > 50:
  print("Great!")
else:
  print("That's ok.")

☐ Great!
☐ 40
☐ That's ok.
☐ Error message

Q: Comparing the else if and the else statement, which one of the following statements is true?

☐ The else statement only applies when all of the else if statements before it are true.

☐ An else condition should not be placed at the end of an if block, but at the start of one.

☐ The else statement checks for specific conditions, whereas the else if statement applies when none of the conditions before it are met.

☐ The else if statements allows for specific conditions, whereas the else statement applies when none of the conditions in the else statements above it are met. x

Q: What is the output of the following code?

grade = 10
nice == False
if grade > 20:
  print("Amazing!")
else:
  if nice == True
    print("That's nice.")
  else:
    print("That's bad.")

☐ That's bad.
☐ That's nice.
☐ Amazing!
☐ 10

LISTS AND LIST FUNCTIONS

Q: What are lists?
- ☐ A list holds items which can be accessed later, starting at an index of 1.
- ☐ A list saves values in a random order.
- ☐ A list is an ordered ranking of numbers.
- ☐ A list contains values which can be accessed by indexes. In a list, the first value is at the index 0.

Q: What is the output of the following code?
preferredItemsList =
["tv", "smartphone", "guitar", "laptop"]
print(preferredItemsList[2])
- ☐ tv
- ☐ smartphone
- ☐ guitar
- ☐ laptop

Q: What is the output of the following code?
preferredItemsList =
["tv", "smartphone", "guitar", "laptop"]
print(preferredItemsList[4])
- ☐ "laptop", since it`s the fourth item in the list.
- ☐ guitar
- ☐ Error message: list index out of range. There is no item at index = 4. The list starts at index = 0 (not 1!), which is the tv.
- ☐ smartphone

Q: Tell Python to print the entire list:
SavedForLater = [film, album, show, episode]
- ☐ print("SavedForLater")
- ☐ print(SavedForLater)
- ☐ print( )
- ☐ print([0])

Q: Additionally to storing strings, lists can also hold integers. What is the output of the following code?
list = [5, 9, 13]
print(list)
- ☐ [5, 9, 13]
- ☐ [5, 9]
- ☐ [5]
- ☐ [13, 9]

Q: What is true of lists?
- ☐ It can only hold data types such as strings and integers.
- ☐ It can hold multiple data types at one, but not integers.
- ☐ It can hold multiple data types at once, but not floats.
- ☐ It can hold multiple data types at once such as integers, strings and floats.

Q: Fill in the x to make this program print "Bear".
zoo = ["Panda", 10, "Bear"]
print(zoo[x])
- ☐ x equals 2
- ☐ x equals 3
- ☐ x equals zoo
- ☐ x equals 0

Q: What function can be used to get the length of a list?
- ☐ leng ( )
- ☐ len( )
- ☐ length ( )
- ☐ lenlist( )

Q: What is the output of the following code?
list = ["bibbidy", "bobbidy", "boo"]
print(len(list))
- ☐ 1
- ☐ 2
- ☐ 3
- ☐ AttributeError: 'list' object has no attribute 'len'.

Q: What function can be used to add a new value to a list?
- ☐ appen( )
- ☐ add ( )
- ☐ adding ( )
- ☐ append ( )

Q: On the other hand, what function can be used to delete a value from a list?
- ☐ pop ( )
- ☐ delete ( )
- ☐ unappend ( )
- ☐ disappear ( )

Q: Deleting a value from our list, what is the output of the second print command?

names = ["Anna", "Belle", "Max", "Jacob"]

print(names)

names.pop([1])

print(names)

- ☐ ["Belle"]
- ☐ ["Anna", "Max", "Jacob"]
- ☐ ["Belle", "Max", "Jacob"]
- ☐ ["Anna"]

Q: Which keyword can be used to test wether a list contains a certain value?

- ☐ inx
- ☐ side
- ☐ out
- ☐ within

Q: What is the output of the following code?

beetroot = ["a", 0, "c"]

print("b" in beetroot]

- ☐ True
- ☐ False
- ☐ b
- ☐ Error

Q: What is the output of the following program?

animals = ["mice", "rats", "cats", "dogs", "zebras", "ferrets"]

print(len(animals))

- ☐ 3
- ☐ 4
- ☐ 5
- ☐ 6

Q: What will be printed to the console?

animals = ["mice", "rats", "cats", "dogs", "zebras", "ferrets"]

if len(animals) == 6

   print(animals[4])

- ☐ IndentationError for the print command
- ☐ Nothing will be printed to the console, as the len conditon is not met.
- ☐ "zebras"
- ☐ "dogs"

Q: Adding and removing values in a list, what is the code output?

animals = ["mice", "rats", "cats", "dogs", "zebras", "ferrets"]

animals.pop(1)

if "rats" in animals:

  print("Call the rat catcher!")

else:

  print("Phew!")

- ☐ Since we removed "rats" from the animals list, the condition is False. Therefore this program prints *Phew!*.
- ☐ Since we removed "rats" from the animals list, the condition is False. Nothing is printed to the console.
- ☐ Since we removed "mice" from the animals list, the condition is True. Therefore this program prints *Call the rat catcher!*.
- ☐ Since we removed "cats" from the animals list, the condition is False. Therefore this program prints *Call the rat catcher!*.

DICTIONARIES AND DICTIONARY FUNCTIONS

Q: What is true of dictionaries?

- ☐ You can fit multiple key-value pairs in a single dictionary, separating them with commas.
- ☐ You can fit multiple key-value pairs in a multiple dictionaries, separating them with semicolon.
- ☐ You can fit one key-value pair per dictionary.
- ☐ You can fit multiple key-value pairs in a single dictionary, separating them with identation.

Q: Which of the following statements about a dictionary in Python are true?

- ☐ A dictionary is a built-in type of object in Python.
- ☐ A dictionary has a limited number of entries.
- ☐ A dictionary can be used to store methods.
- ☐ A dictionary always needs to be imported first.

Q: How can you access a value in a dictionary?

- ☐ You can access it using its value.
- ☐ You can access it using its key.
- ☐ You can access it using its pair.
- ☐ You can access it using its function.

Q: In the following example, what needs to be inserted in X to have Python print the value "Go"?

goal = {"Let": "Go"}
habit = goal[X]
print(habit)

☐   X needs to be "2".
☐   X needs ti be "habit".
☐   X needs to be "Let".
☐   X needs to be "Go".

Q: Knowing you can also overwrite existing values in a dictionary, what is the output of the following code?

goal = {"Let": "Go"}
goal ["Let"] = "Do"
print(goal)

☐   {'Let': 'Let'}
☐   {'Do': 'Let'}
☐   {'Let': 'Go'}
☐   {'Do': 'Go'}

Q: When you compare lists and dictionaries, what is one of the main differences between these two?

☐   Dictionaries hold values while lists do not.
☐   Lists hold values while dictionaries do not.
☐   Lists use keys while dictionaries use indexes.
☐   Dictionaries use keys while lists use indexes.

Q: What is the output of the following program?

seven = {'one': 1, 'two': 2, 'three': 3, 'four': 4}
print(seven['two']

☐   3
☐   2
☐   1
☐   four

Q: What is the output of the following program?

seven = {'one': 1, 'two': 2, 'three': 3, 'four': 4}
print(seven['two']

☐   3
☐   2
☐   1
☐   four

Q: What is the function with which you can see all of the keys in a dictionary?
- ☐ keys( )
- ☐ values( )
- ☐ allkeys( )
- ☐ allvalues( )

Q: How can you print all the keys in the dictionary "names"?
- ☐ names.keys( )
- ☐ names.keys
- ☐ keys(names)
- ☐ keys( ).names

Q: How can you check if a dictionary contains a certain key?
- ☐ contain
- ☐ out
- ☐ in
- ☐ from

Q: Also, how can you update multiple values at once?
- ☐ overwrite( )
- ☐ update( )
- ☐ reinsert( )
- ☐ refresh( )

Q: You need to remove a value from a dictionary. How do you do this?
- ☐ By using the function delete( ) and specifying which key to remove.
- ☐ By using the function out( ) and specifying which key to remove.
- ☐ By using the function remove( ) and specifying which key to remove.
- ☐ By using the function pop( ) and specifying which key to remove.

Q: How do you delete the key-value pair with key 'Same' from a dictionary 'Songs'?
- ☐ Songs.delete('Same')
- ☐ Songs.pop('Same')
- ☐ remove(Songs, 'Same')
- ☐ delete(Songs, 'Same')

Q: What is the advantage of using loops?

☐ Loops act as brackets around similar functions.

☐ Using loops, you can avoid writing the exact same line of code several times and therefore remove duplication.

☐ Without loops, Python doesn't work through identical lines of code.

☐ Loops serve as functions within repeated statements.

Q: What is the output of the following code?

for i in range(3):

   print(i)

      0

☐ 1

   2

☐ i

☐ range(3)

☐ 3

Q: When looking at the line "for i in n", what does i stand for?

☐ The loop variable i takes on the countervalues of the loop.

☐ The loop variable i equals to the function values before the loop.

☐ The loop variable i equals n.

☐ The loop variable i in the loop takes on each value in whatever the loop is iterating over.

Q: Is it mandatory to use the "i" in loops?

☐ No, it is not. Loop variables can be names however we like, including reservec keywords.

☐ No, it is not. Loop variables can be named however we like, except for reserved keywords.

☐ Yes, it is mandatory. If named otherwise, Python will not detect the loop.

☐ It depends on the Python version used.

Q: What is the output of this code?

breeds = ["bulldog", "terrier", "foxhound"]

for cat in breeds:

   print(cat)

☐ Syntax Error, since cats are not dog breeds.

☐ cat

☐ Syntax Error, since the loop variable i hasn't been used.

   bulldog

☐ terrier

   foxhound

Q: What is the output of this code?
breeds = ["bulldog", "terrier", "foxhound"]

for for in breeds:
  print(for)
- ☐ Syntax Error: invalid syntax since for is a reserved keyword.
- ☐ Syntax Error: invalid syntax due to duplication of the word 'for'.
  bulldog
- ☐ terrier
  foxhound
- ☐ It will print the word 'for' since it is a reserved keyword.

Q: How many times does this program print "Nice to meet you!"?
n = ["n", "b", "c"]
for i in n:
  print("Nice to meet you!")
- ☐ "Nice to meet you!" is printed two times since the index starts at 0.
- ☐ "Nice to meet you!" is printed three times since there are 3 elements in the list n.
- ☐ "Nice to meet you!" is not printed at all since it is not part of the list.
- ☐ SyntaxError: invalid syntax since n is a reserved keyword.

Q: What is the output of this program?
m = ""
for i in range(3):
  m = m + str(i)
print(m)
- ☐ i
- ☐ 123
- ☐ 3
- ☐ 012

Q: We've looked at for loops. What is true for while loops?
- ☐ A while loop executes code only when its condition is false.
- ☐ A while loop stops when its condition is true.
- ☐ A while loop executes code as long as its condition is true.
- ☐ A while loop doesn't depent on conditions.

Q: How many times will the following while loop print "number"?

number = 3
while number > 0:
   print(number)
   number = number -1

☐   Once: -1.
☐   Twice: 3, 2, then stop because number = 0.
☐   Three times: 3, 2, 1, then stop because number = 0.
☐   Four times: 3, 2, 1, 0, then stop because number = 0.

Q: What is the keyword called used to exit out of a while loop?
☐   break
☐   stop
☐   out
☐   exit

Q: What does Python print to the console?

bun = 0
while True:
   if bun == 8:
      break
   else:
      bun += 1
   print(bun)

☐   bun
☐   1, 2, 3, 4, 5, 6, 7, 8
☐   8
☐   False

Q: Now with the right condition, while loops can become infinite. What about this one?

z = 0
while z >= 0:
   print("Infinity")
   z += 1

☐   It is finite, since z only adds 1 after printing the word "Infinity".
☐   It cannot be finite, since there is not break keyword in the code.
☐   It is infinite, since z will always be greater than 0 due to the z +=1 line.
☐   It is finite, because the condition will turn out False.

Advanced Python

Tools

Q: What is an easier way to add up numbers without using a for loop?
- ☐ Combining two for loops.
- ☐ Using the sum() function.
- ☐ Adding numbers using +=.
- ☐ There is no easier way.

Q: Which of the following statements *is true* for the sum() function?
- ☐ It can sum up integers and floats, but not complex numbers.
- ☐ It can sum up integers, floats and complex numbers, but it will always output an integer.
- ☐ It can only sum up integers.
- ☐ It can sum up integers, floats and complex numbers.

Q: Which function allows me to easily access a sequence of integers in Python?
- ☐ Using the range() function will output every integer between start and stop -1.
- ☐ Using the range() function will output every integer between start -1 and stop -1.
- ☐ Using the range() function will output every integer between start -1 and stop.
- ☐ Using the range() function will output every integer between start and stop.

Q: What happens if the range() function only contains a stop integer?
- ☐ A syntax error will appear.
- ☐ Python will assume the range to start from 0.
- ☐ It will only output the stop integer.
- ☐ Python will assume the range to start from 1.

Q: Chaning an existing value can be done using assignments like +=. For example, A +=
B is equivalent to A = A + B. What other assignments are valid?
- ☐ *=
- ☐ /=
- ☐ -=
- ☐ #=

Q: What happens when you use int() on a float?
- ☐ It rounds up or down everything after the decimal point.
- ☐ It will add a "0" after the first decimal place.
- ☐ It just cuts off everything after the decimal point.
- ☐ It will output a syntax error.

Q: What happens when you use round() on a float?
- ☐ It rounds up or down everything after the decimal point.
- ☐ It will add a "0" after the first decimal place.
- ☐ It just cuts off everything after the decimal point.
- ☐ It will output a syntax error.

Q: What is the correct way to write the range() function?
- ☐ a = range(2, 5)
- ☐ a : range[2, 5]
- ☐ a = range(2; 5)
- ☐ a = range[2: 5]

INDEXING

Q: What can you do by using indexing with ":"?
- ☐ Sum up ranges.
- ☐ See ranges of strings and lists.
- ☐ Calculating new values.
- ☐ Changing existing values.

Q: Which one of these lines will output the whole string *str = "this is not a pipe"*?
- ☐ str[all]
- ☐ str[0:17]
- ☐ str[0:2]
- ☐ str[0:len(str)]

Q: What happens if you leave out a value for the beginning or end of a range?
- ☐ Python will ask where you want to start / end.
- ☐ Python will output a syntax error.
- ☐ Python will assume you want to start at the start or end of the string/list.
- ☐ Python will assume you want to start at the start +1 and end -1 of the string/list.

Q: Given the list *four_ears = ["relationship", "self-revelation", "factual", "appeal"],* which of these will give out the last two list elements ["factual", "appeal"]?
- ☐ four_ears[:2]
- ☐ four_ears[2:]
- ☐ four_ears[:]
- ☐ four_ears[0:3]

Q: Assuming we have a list of strings *four_ears = ["relationship", "self-revelation", "factual", "appeal"],* how can we find the first letter of the third string?
- ☐ four_ears[1][3]
- ☐ four_ears[0][2]
- ☐ four_ears[3][0]
- ☐ four_ears[2][0]

Q: Given this line of code *hello_there = "obi wan kenobi"*, which one of the following does not return the whole string "obi wan kenobi"?

- ☐ hello_there[0:len(hello_there)-1]
- ☐ hello_there[:]
- ☐ hello_there[0:len(hello_there)]
- ☐ hello_there[0:]

Q: Given this line of code *snippets = ["we will rock", "there is no", "there you go"]*, which one of the following lines of code will output "we will rock you"?

- ☐ first = snippets[0]
  second = snippets[2][1]
  print(first + second)
- ☐ first = snippets[1]
  second = snippets[0][2]
  print(first + second)
- ☐ first = snippets[2]
  second = snippets[3][1]
  print(first + second)
- ☐ first = snippets[3]
  second = snippets[1][2]
  print(first + second)

FUNCTIONS

Q: How can we define our own function with the name "music"?

- ☐ def music:
- ☐ Def Music
- ☐ def: music
- ☐ def music ( ):

Q: You can also define a function which does nothing, for instance if you want to change it later. What is the keyword for that?

- ☐ do nothing
- ☐ pass
- ☐ don't
- ☐ nothing

Q: What happens if we make a variable outside a function but then try giving it a different value inside the function's identation?

- ☐ The value of the function doesn't change.
- ☐ Python asks which value to use.
- ☐ The value of the function changes.
- ☐ Python outputs an error.

Q: What ist the output of the following code?

```
nice = True
def so_great():
    nice = False
so_great()
print(nice)
```

☐ nice
☐ so_great
☐ False
☐ True

Q: Which one of these statements about functions is *not true*?
☐ We can store what a function returns in a variable.
☐ Functions perform the code indented inside them.
☐ We cannot use while loops inside of functions.
☐ We can write functions inside of functions.

Q: What is the output of these lines?

```
def yes_four( ):
    answer = "yes"
    for i in range(4):
        print(yes_four)
```

☐ One time the word "yes".
☐ It prints the string "yes_four".
☐ These lines output an error.
☐ Four times the word "yes".

Q: What is the output of the following code?

```
z = 10
def z_new( ):
    z = 20
    return z
x = z_new()
print(x == 20 and z == 10)
```

☐ 30
☐ x and z
☐ True
☐ z_new

Q: Functions can take inputs which are arguments and go in the parentheses after the function name. What is the output of the following function with the argument "sports":
def always_time_for (sports):
   *return 2 * sports*
always_time_for(2)
☐   2
☐   4
☐   sport sports
☐   2sports

Q: It is possible to put anything into a function. However, what is the drawback when using operations that only work on specific types?
☐   Python won't allow for other arguments in a function.
☐   We cannot use any other functions.
☐   We limit the arguments of our function to those types.
☐   Functions become restricted to a certain number of arguments.

Q: What is a docstring?
☐   It is a multi-line string which can be written inside functions in order to explain what the function does and what its arguments should be.
☐   It is a string used to address documents outside of the console.
☐   It is a single-linge string which will help check for errors in your code before running it.
☐   It is a special string that allows you to find any keyword entered after the word "doc".

Q: Which symbol begins a docstring?
☐   //
☐   =!
☐   \\
☐   """

Q: What is the function that helps with finding out about a specific function?
☐   explain()
☐   assist()
☐   help()
☐   support()

Q: What is the output of the following code?

```
def welcome(name):
    ''' Takes a string and prints a welcome message.'''
    print("Welcome, " + name)

help(welcome)
```

☐ Welcome, name
☐ Takes a string and prints a welcome message.
☐ Syntax error
☐ welcome(name)

Q: Instead of using a docstring, you can also prevent bad inputs to functions by…?
☐ …making the function as complex as possible.
☐ …letting Python tell the user what to do by giving cryptic error messages.
☐ …telling the user what to do instead by using the print command, e.g. print("x must be a float!").
☐ …giving the number of first level support to the user before even running the code.

Q: What is the output of the following code when z equals "x"?

```
def particle(z):
    return z * z
```

☐ Error, as we can't multiply strings.
☐ z
☐ z^2
☐ zz

RECURSION

Q: How can you describe recursion?
☐ Recursion is using a function inside of another function.
☐ Recursion is a variable used to form a loop.
☐ Recursion is defining an argument which is continually applied.
☐ Recursion is calling a function inside of itself, usually using a base case and a recursive step.

Q: What are typical use cases for recursion?
☐ Factorials (an integer multiplied by every integer less than it down to 0) and Fibonacci numbers (the first two are 1 and all the others are found by adding the numbers before them).
☐ If and else statements.
☐ Methods and arguments.
☐ Dictionaries and loops.

Q: What is the output of the following code?

```
def factorial(x):
    if x == 1:          # base case
        return x
    else:               # recursive step
        return x * factorial(x-1)

factorial(3)
```

☐   3
☐   4
☐   5
☐   6

Q: What is the output of the following lines of code?

```
def fibonacci(z):
    if z == 1 or z == 2:    # base case
        return 1
    else:                   # recursive step
        return fib(z-1) + fib(n-2)

fibonacci(4)
```

☐   3
☐   4
☐   5
☐   6

Q: When does it make sense to use recursion?
☐   When we want to calculate a function inside of another function.
☐   When we have to compute something similar over and over for many different inputs.
☐   When we want to overwrite an existing function.
☐   When we are not sure how to define the arguments of a function.

CLASSES

Q: Python allows for more flexibility than just built-in types. What is the keyword used to define own objects?
- ☐ def
- ☐ own
- ☐ category
- ☐ class

Q: Having defined a new class, how do you tell Python to make an object of that class?
- ☐ Using the function __init__().
- ☐ Using the function __init__:
- ☐ Using the function _init_()
- ☐ Using the function init:

Q: Classes can have attributes. But what are attributes?
- ☐ Attributes are functions used to overwrite existing arguments.
- ☐ Attributes are stored properties which can be accessed and changed.
- ☐ Attributes allow for indexes to be drawn upon.
- ☐ Attributes are the last part of if and else statements.

Q: How can you access existing attributes defined in the class definition?
- ☐ By using a . after the object's name.
- ☐ By using the function *get*.
- ☐ By printing the attribute.
- ☐ By calling the right index within the class.

Q: What is the output of the following code?
class Sunny:
  a = 5
  b = 10
  def __init__(self):
    pass
z = Point()
print(z.a)
z.a = 1
print(z.b)

- ☐ a
  b
- ☐ Error message for not using the *get* function to call on the attributes a and b.
- ☐ 5
  10
- ☐ Point.5

Q: Setting attributes is also possible by making them arguments to the __init__()
function. What is the benefit of doing this though?
- ☐ This way, they can be called upon more easily by using the *get* function.
- ☐ The __init__() function sets these attributes as a default throughout the code.
- ☐ The use of the __init__() function operates as a trigger to those arguments.
- ☐ This way, you can set them at the same time when creating a new object.

Q: What is the output of the following code?

```
class Song:
    def __init__(self, title, artist):
    self.title = title
    self.artist = artist

play = Song("Imagine", "John Lennon")
print(play.title)
```

- ☐ "Imagine"
- ☐ "John Lennon"
- ☐ "Song"
- ☐ "Title"

Q: In Python, what is a method?
- ☐ A method is a means to print to the console.
- ☐ A method is a statements inside of a function.
- ☐ A method is a function inside of a class.
- ☐ A method is an argument inside of an else statement

Q: What has to be the first argument for any method?
- ☐ this
- ☐ that
- ☐ mine
- ☐ self

Q: What is the correct way to call on a method?
- ☐ Using a . after the object's name.
- ☐ Using a " before the object's name.
- ☐ Using a m after the object's name.
- ☐ Using a * before the object's name.

Q: How can you describe inheritance?
- ☐ When closing a class, its attributes are given to the next class in the code.
- ☐ When having multiple classes that have attributes in common, we can build a general class and then make more specific derived classes.
- ☐ When looking at three classes, one class will receive particular characteristics from the other two.
- ☐ When having a class that impacts other classes in close proximity to it.

Q: Looking at the following code, which one is the base class and which ones are the more specific classes?

```
class Animals:
    def __init__(self, type, name):
        self.type = type
        self.name = name

    def change_type(self, type):
        self.type = type

    def change_name(self, name):
        self.name = name
```

- ☐ The first two classes are the base classes and the last one is the more speific class.
- ☐ The second class ("change_type") is the base class and the other two are the more specific classes.
- ☐ The last class ("change_name") is the base class and the other two are the more specific classes.
- ☐ The first class ("__init__") is the base class and the following two are the more specific classes.

Q: How can we make a derived class?
- ☐ Put the name of the derived class in brackets.
- ☐ Put the name of the base class in parentheses.
- ☐ Put the name of the base class behind the derived class separated by a dot.
- ☐ Put the name of the derived class behind the base class separated by a dot.

Q: What is the output of the following code?

```
class Parent(Family):
    pass

dad = Parent("Jack", 42)
dad.change_age(43)
print(dad.age)
```

- ☐ 42
- ☐ "Jack"
- ☐ 43
- ☐ "Parent"

Q: Having defined an initializer, what about adding more attributes and methods to derived classes?

- ☐ More attributes and methods can be added to derived classes to store specific things where they are different from other dervied classes.
- ☐ You can only add one attribute or method at a time and it has to be in a specific order.
- ☐ Once a class has been initialized, there is no adding of additional attributes and methods afterwards.
- ☐ Classes do not contain attributes and methods.

Q: Which one of the following statements is not true?

- ☐ There can be as many levels of base and derviced classes as wanted.
- ☐ The derived classes inherit all the methods of its base class.
- ☐ With inheritance, we can make related classes without having to repeat code.
- ☐ We cannot add any additional attributes to derived classes.

MODULES

Q: What are modules?
- ☐ Modules are objects which have unique attributes and behavior.
- ☐ Modules are libraries of functions, values and classes which can be used in individual programs.
- ☐ Modules are self-contained units within lines of code.
- ☐ Modules are chunks of IT architecture code is built around.

Q: The module math is a very useful one, for example when calculating the square root of a variable. However, we don't want to repeat syntax. How can be bypass having to use the math.sqrt() function repeatedly?
- ☐ We can write a class where the function is renamed to a shorter name.
- ☐ We can write a function wich repeats the line of codes for how often needed.
- ☐ We can use recursion on importing modules.
- ☐ We can use the keyword "as" so we can refer to the module using a shorter name.

Q: What is the output of the following code?
import math as m
m.sqrt(16)
- ☐ 4
- ☐ 2
- ☐ 8
- ☐ 10

Q: Knowing you only need a few functions from a module, how could you import just these few functions and avoid the "." syntax altogether?
- ☐ By using the keyword in, e.g. *in math import cos*
- ☐ By using the keyword out, e.g. *out math import cos*
- ☐ By using the keyword from, e.g. *from math import cos*
- ☐ By using the keyword of, e.g. *of math import cos*

Q: If you're not sure what functions from a module are needed and you would like to import everything within a module, how can you do this?
- ☐ By using *, e.g. *from math import **
- ☐ By using the keyword all, e.g. *from math import all*
- ☐ By using (), e.g. *from math import ()*
- ☐ By using the keyword complete, e.g. *complete import from math*

Q: How can you access information on specific module functions?

☐ The print(help) function gives information on what's printed to the console.

☐ The help() function will give information on any imported functions.

☐ Read the documentation or ask first level support.

☐ Information is automatically given when importing the module functions.

Q: How can you import multiple modules?

☐ By listing them separated by a comma, e.g. *import math, random.*

☐ By listing them separated by a semicolon, e.g. *import math; random.*

☐ By writing them inside of parentheses, e.g. *import(math, random).*

The only way to import multiple modules is by importing them separately, e.g.

☐ *import math*
import random

Q: What does the module random do?

☐ It has functions for doing random unit tests.

☐ It has functions for randomly debugging code.

☐ It has functions for generating random arguments in classes.

☐ It has functions for choosing numbers randomly.

Q: What is the output of the following code?

import math, random

 # pick a number between 1 and 20

number = random.randint(1, 20)

math.sqrt(number)

☐ The square root of the number chosen by the user.

☐ Syntax error.

☐ The square root of the randomly picked number between 1 and 20.

☐ 5

Q: What does the module datetime do?

☐ It calculates time zones for different countries.

☐ It gives back the current date and time.

☐ It contains the calendar of the last five years.

☐ It contains functions for working with times and dates.

Q: What is the output of the following lines of code?

```
import random
def throw_dices():
    dice_one = random.randint(1,6)
    dice_two = random.randint(1,6)
    return dice_one + dice_two
```

☐   This code will return the first dice roll.
☐   This code will return first one, then the other dice roll.
☐   This code will return the sum of two dice rolls.
☐   This code will return the second dice roll.

Q: Which of the following import statements is not valid?

a) import math
*b) from math import ***
c) import sin from math
d) import math as m

☐   a
☐   b
☐   c
☐   d

Q: What does this function do?

```
from dateime import *
def day_until 2022(day):
    countdown = date(2022, 1, 1)
    time = countdown – day
    return time.days
```

☐   This function returns the years until 2022.
☐   This function subtracts the days passed.
☐   This function calculates the age I will be on January 1, 2022.
☐   This function counts down to January 1, 2022.

ANSWERS

BASIC PYTHON

PRINTING

Q: What does the print() function do?
- ☐ It tells the printer to print any open document using the default printer.
- ☐ It helps to debug printing errors.
- ☐ It allows to look for bugs in the code by printing bugfree parts.
- ☐ **It displays things to the console.**

Q: Which of these command lines will print "Hello World"?
- ☐ say("Hello World!")
- ☐ print:("Hello World!")
- ☐ output:(("Hello World!"))
- ☐ **print("Hello World!") – watch out for the right syntax.**

Q: What's the command print() in Python?
- ☐ **A function**
- ☐ A list
- ☐ A variable
- ☐ An array

Q: Which of the following examples for the print() function *does not* lead to an error output?
- ☐ **print(5)**
- ☐ **print(„foo")**
- ☐ **print(True)**
- ☐ print:self → SyntaxError: Missing parentheses in call to 'print'.

Q: What is the output of multiple print() functions? E.g. these:
print ("I love my ")
print ("dog!")
- ☐ "I love my dog!"
- ☐ Python doesn't work with multiple print() functions, it will output an error.
- ☐ **I love my**
  dog!
- ☐ It will print only "I love my " and stop there.

STRINGS

1. Q: Which one of these is a string?
    - ☐ **"you"**
    - ☐ <are>
    - ☐ *so*
    - ☐ ;right;

Q: How can you add whitespaces in between combined strings?
- ☐ print ("That's" + whitespace + "true!")
- ☐ **print ("That's" + " " + "true!")**
- ☐ print ("That's" + < > + "true!")
- ☐ print ("That's" + __ + "true!")

Q: Sometimes, you want to know the number of characters in a string. What's the name of the function that will return the length of a string?
- ☐ num()
- ☐ length()
- ☐ **len()**
- ☐ count()

Q: What is the output of this code:
print(len("Hello world!"))
- ☐ syntax error due to double brackets.
- ☐ 10, as whitepsaces and special characters are not counted.
- ☐ **12, as all characters within the quotation marks are counted.**
- ☐ 14, as all characters within the brackets are counted.

Q: Let's look at added lengths of strings: What is the output of this code:
print(len("Nice") + len("job!"))
- ☐ 8
- ☐ 7
- ☐ 6
- ☐ 5

Q: How can you identify a string?
- ☐ They are always surrounded by brackets.
- ☐ They are always inside of functions.
- ☐ **They are always surrounded by single or double quotation marks.**
- ☐ They are always written in italic.

Q: How can you display a string to the console?

☐ This is not possible.

☐ Use the function len().

☐ Write strings in italic.

☑ **Use the function print().**

Q: What is the output of this code?

print(len("Well") + ("done!"))

☐ 7

☐ 8

☑ **9**

☐ 10

VARIABLES

Q: What are variables in Python?

☐ Variables are a set of attributes.

☐ Variables are symbols that represents a quantity.

☑ **Variables store values in a name so that the name can later be used to refer to the value.**

☐ Variables are a way to display things to the console.

Q: What is the output of this code?

animal = "dormouse"

print(animal)

☐ animal

☑ **dormouse**

☐ error: invalid syntax

☐ print

Q: Combining different variables, what is the output of this code?

cat = "tom"

mouse = "jerry"

print(cat + mouse)

☑ **tomjerry**

☐ tom+jerry

☐ tom jerry

☐ jerrytom

Q: What happens in this case?

print(animal)

animal = "fox"

☐ Python prints fox to the console, as animal = fox.

☐ Python prints animal to the console, as this is the first command line.

☐ Python prints nothing.

☐ **Python prints an error message saying the name "animal" is not defined.**

Q: Variables can be updated by setting them to a new value. What is the output of the following code?

animal = "Shellfish"

animal = "Octopus"

print(animal)

☐ **Octopus**

☐ Nothing

☐ Shellfish

☐ animal

Q: When naming the variables, use a descriptive name and avoid using operators. What are invalid variable names?

☐ =

☐ *

☐ +

☐ **animal**

Q: What is the main benefit of using variables?

☐ **Variables use the same value in many places.**

☐ Variables use many values in the same place.

☐ Variables store many values in a single name.

☐ Variables set many names to the same value.

NUMBERS

Q: What are the different types of numbers in Python?
- ☐ **Integers**
- ☐ Strings
- ☐ **Floats**
- ☐ Signs

Q: What are integers?
- ☐ Numbers with a decimal point like 1.125.
- ☐ **Whole numbers like 2, 6 or -80.**
- ☐ Special characters like ?, ! or #.
- ☐ Numbers in percent, like 75%.

Q: Sometimes, it is helpful to convert a string to a number. What function does this?
- ☐ num()
- ☐ str()
- ☐ **int()**
- ☐ con()

Q: What is printed to the console?
y = int("2")
print(y)
- ☐ **2**
- ☐ "2"
- ☐ y
- ☐ "y"

Q: What is the output of this code?
int("Hello world!")
- ☐ "Hello world"
- ☐ **ValueError: invalid literal for int()**
- ☐ 12
- ☐ SyntaxError: invalid syntax

Q: Converting a string to a number, what does Python print to the console?
text = "12"
print(int(text))
- ☐ **The number 12**
- ☐ The string "12"
- ☐ The string "text"
- ☐ ValueError: invalid literal for int()

Q: Using numbers in Python, it is possible to calculate with them? What is the output of this code?

x = 2
y = 4
z = x + y
print(z)

- ☐ 2
- ☐ 4
- ☐ **6**
- ☐ 8

Q: So we can add numbers in Python. What else can we calculate?

- ☐ **multiply values using ***
- ☐ **subtract values using -**
- ☐ **divide values using /**
- ☐ we can calculate nothing else

Q: What is the output of this code?

x = 60
y = 2
z = (x + y)/y
print(z)

- ☐ 21
- ☐ **31**
- ☐ 41
- ☐ 51

Q: What is the output of this code?

zodiac = 100
sign = 4
print((zodiac*sign)+(zodiac/sign))

- ☐ **425**
- ☐ 4
- ☐ 104
- ☐ 208

BOOLEANS

Q: A boolean is a value which can be:
- ☐ Right
- ☐ **True**
- ☐ Wrong
- ☐ **False**

Q: What are the values True and False equivalent to in Python?
- ☐ 0 and 1
- ☐ **1 and 0**
- ☐ 2 and 1
- ☐ 1 and 2

Q: If True equals 1 and False equals 0, what is the output of this code?
light = False
darkness = 0
print(light == 0)
- ☐ False
- ☐ **True**
- ☐ 0
- ☐ light

Q: What does Python print to the console?
code = False
print(int(code))
- ☐ **0**
- ☐ 1
- ☐ 2
- ☐ 3

Q: What does Python print to the console?
code = False
print(bool(code))
- ☐ 0
- ☐ **False**
- ☐ True
- ☐ 1

Q: What are the different boolean operators?
- ☐ **and**
- ☐ so
- ☐ **or**
- ☐ **not**

Q: Boolean values can be combined using and 'and' operator. True and True equals True. What equals True and False?
- ☐ Also True.
- ☐ Error message due to contradicting booleans.
- ☐ **False.**
- ☐ Nothing is printed to the console because it can't be compiled.

Q: What is the output when using the 'or' operator in this case: True or False?
- ☐ **True.**
- ☐ True and False.
- ☐ False.
- ☐ Nothing is printed to the console because it can't be compiled.

Q: Using the operator 'not' to negate a boolean value, what is the result of 'not False'?
- ☐ **True.**
- ☐ Not False.
- ☐ False.
- ☐ Nothing is printed to the console because it can't be compiled.

Q: Making a boolean value the opposite of whatever it currently is, what is the output of the following code?
warm = True
cold = not warm
print(cold)
- ☐ cold
- ☐ cot warm
- ☐ **False**
- ☐ True

Q: Put your boolean operators to the test: what is the single boolean value of e?
c = True
d = False
e = (c or d) and (c and d)
- ☐ **False**
- ☐ True
- ☐ True and False
- ☐ False and True

Q: What do if statements do?
- ☐ They allow a Python program to choose from multiple options.
- ☐ They allow a Python program to compile the code.
- ☐ **They allow a Python program to make decisions based on boolean expressions.**
- ☐ They allow a Python program to infer values from variables.

Q: What would Python print to the console according to the following code?
warm = True
if warm == False:
  print("It's cold.")
- ☐ It's cold.
- ☐ warm
- ☐ False
- ☐ **Nothing is printed to the console, since warm is not equal to False.**

Q: How does the if statement exactly work?
- ☐ **The code following the keyword 'if' has to be a boolean expression. If the expression evaluates to be True, then the code in the if statement will be executed.**
- ☐ The code has to contain the 'if' keyword but doesn't need to be True to be executed.
- ☐ The expression needs to equal to True, but also works without the 'if' keyword.
- ☐ The boolean expression needs to equal to False or otherwise the if statement won't work.

Q: Applying multiple if statements, what does Python print to the console?
height = 20
if height >= 10:
  print("medium")
if height >= 20:
  print("tall")
- ☐ It will print only "medium".
- ☐ It will print only "tall".
- ☐ It will print the height, so "20".
- ☐ **It will print both words, since both if statements are met, so:**
  medium
  tall

Q: Combining different conditions, what does Python print to the console?

temp = 8
cold = 0
sunshine = False
rain = True
if rain == sunshine or (temp < cold):
  print("No thank you.")
if temp > cold:
  print("Alright.")

- ☐ **It will print "Alright.", since rain doesn't equal sunshine and temp isn't less than cold.**
- ☐ It will print "No thank you.", since the operator used is 'or'.
- ☐ Syntax error: There can't be both a False and a True value defined before an if statement.
- ☐ It will print print nothing to the console, since neither one of the conditions is true.

ELSE IF AND ELSE

Q: Why does it make sense to use an else if statement?
- ☐ **Instead of using multiple if statements, it can be used chaining multiple conditions together.**
- ☐ It allows for a second, third or fourth if statement after having used a first one.
- ☐ It only makes sense to use an else if statement if there is anything else to write.
- ☐ Multiple if statements testing different conditions are always better than else if statements.

Q: What is the keyword used for writing an else if statement?
- ☐ elseif
- ☐ ifel
- ☐ **elif**
- ☐ else-if

Q: What is the output of this code?

warm = 20

if warm > 30:
  print("very warm")
if warm > 20:
  print("warm")
if warm > 10:
  print("pleasant")

- ☐ 10
- ☐ warm
- ☐ **pleasant**
- ☐ 20

Q: In a code where the first if condition is True, what happens to the other else if condition?

- ☐ It will be checked regardless of the first condition.
- ☐ **It will be ignored since the first condition is True.**
- ☐ It will be checked against the first condition.
- ☐ The first condition needs to be False so that the second condition gets checked.

Q: What is the output of this code?

length = 1

if length > 10:
  print("longest")
if length > 1:
  print("long")
if length < 1 :
  print("short")

- ☐ **It will print nothing to the console, since < and > means that the value needs to be either smaller or greater.**
- ☐ long
- ☐ short
- ☐ shortest

Q: What is true of the else if condition?

- ☐ **You cannot start with an else if statement, it needs to come after an if statement.**
- ☐ You can start with an else if statement.
- ☐ More than one else if statement will lead to an error.
- ☐ More than five else if statements will lead to a runtime error.

Q: You can add an else condition to the end of an if block. What does this mean for the execution of the if statements?

- ☐ The code in the else block will be executed only if the condition in the if statement before it is true.
- ☐ **If the condition in the if statement before the else condition is false, the code in the else block will be executed.**
- ☐ Both the if statement and the else statement will be executed.
- ☐ If you add an else statement, the if statement before that will be ignored.

Q: What is the output of the following code?

grade = 40
if grade > 50:
  print("Great!")
else:
  print("That's ok.")

- ☐ Great!
- ☐ 40
- ☐ **That's ok.**
- ☐ Error message

Q: Comparing the else if and the else statement, which one of the following statements is true?

- ☐ The else statement only applies when all of the else if statements before it are true.
- ☐ An else condition should not be placed at the end of an if block, but at the start of one.
- ☐ The else statement checks for specific conditions, whereas the else if statement applies when none of the conditions before it are met.
- ☐ **The else if statements allows for specific conditions, whereas the else statement applies when none of the conditions in the else statements above it are met.**

Q: What is the output of the following code?

grade = 10
nice == False
if grade > 20:
  print("Amazing!")
else:
  if nice == True
    print("That's nice.")
  else:
    print("That's bad.")

- ☐ **That's bad.**
- ☐ That's nice.
- ☐ Amazing!
- ☐ 10

LISTS AND LIST FUNCTIONS

Q: What are lists?
- ☐ A list holds items which can be accessed later, starting at an index of 1.
- ☐ A list saves values in a random order.
- ☐ A list is an ordered ranking of numbers.
- ☐ **A list contains values which can be accessed by indexes. In a list, the first value is at the index 0.**

Q: What is the output of the following code?
preferredItemsList =
["tv", "smartphone", "guitar", "laptop"]
print(preferredItemsList[2])
- ☐ tv
- ☐ smartphone
- ☐ **guitar**
- ☐ laptop

Q: What is the output of the following code?
preferredItemsList =
["tv", "smartphone", "guitar", "laptop"]
print(preferredItemsList[4])
- ☐ "laptop", since it`s the fourth item in the list.
- ☐ guitar
- ☐ **Error message: list index out of range. There is no item at index = 4. The list starts at index = 0 (not 1!), which is the tv.**
- ☐ smartphone

Q: Tell Python to print the entire list:
SavedForLater = [film, album, show, episode]
- ☐ print("SavedForLater")
- ☐ **print(SavedForLater)**
- ☐ print( )
- ☐ print([0])

Q: Additionally to storing strings, lists can also hold integers. What is the output of the following code?
list = [5, 9, 13]
print(list)
- ☐ **[5, 9, 13]**
- ☐ [5, 9]
- ☐ [5]
- ☐ [13, 9]

Q: What is true of lists?
- ☐ It can only hold data types such as strings and integers.
- ☐ It can hold multiple data types at one, but not integers.
- ☐ It can hold multiple data types at once, but not floats.
- ☐ **It can hold multiple data types at once such as integers, strings and floats.**

Q: Fill in the x to make this program print "Bear".
zoo = ["Panda", 10, "Bear"]
print(zoo[x])
- ☐ **x equals 2**
- ☐ x equals 3
- ☐ x equals zoo
- ☐ x equals 0

Q: What function can be used to get the length of a list?
- ☐ leng ( )
- ☐ **len( )**
- ☐ length ( )
- ☐ lenlist( )

Q: What is the output of the following code?
list = ["bibbidy", "bobbidy", "boo"]
print(len(list))
- ☐ 1
- ☐ 2
- ☐ **3**
- ☐ AttributeError: 'list' object has no attribute 'len'.

Q: What function can be used to add a new value to a list?
- ☐ appen( )
- ☐ add ( )
- ☐ adding ( )
- ☐ **append ( )**

Q: On the other hand, what function can be used to delete a value from a list?
- ☐ **pop ( )**
- ☐ delete ( )
- ☐ unappend ( )
- ☐ disappear ( )

Q: Deleting a value from our list, what is the output of the second print command?

names = ["Anna", "Belle", "Max", "Jacob"]
print(names)
names.pop([1])
print(names)

- ☐ ["Belle"]
- ☐ **["Anna", "Max", "Jacob"]**
- ☐ ["Belle", "Max", "Jacob"]
- ☐ ["Anna"]

Q: Which keyword can be used to test wether a list contains a certain value?

- ☐ **in**
- ☐ side
- ☐ out
- ☐ within

Q: What is the output of the following code?

beetroot = ["a", 0, "c"]
print("b" in beetroot]

- ☐ True
- ☐ **False**
- ☐ b
- ☐ Error

Q: What is the output of the following program?

animals = ["mice", "rats", "cats", "dogs", "zebras", "ferrets"]
print(len(animals))

- ☐ 3
- ☐ 4
- ☐ 5
- ☐ **6**

Q: What will be printed to the console?

animals = ["mice", "rats", "cats", "dogs", "zebras", "ferrets"]
if len(animals) == 6
   print(animals[4])

- ☐ IndentationError for the print command
- ☐ Nothing will be printed to the console, as the len conditon is not met.
- ☐ **"zebras"**
- ☐ "dogs"

Q: Adding and removing values in a list, what is the code output?
animals = ["mice", "rats", "cats", "dogs", "zebras", "ferrets"]
animals.pop(1)
if "rats" in animals:
  print("Call the rat catcher!")
else:
  print("Phew!")

- ☐ **Since we removed "rats" from the animals list, the condition is False. Therefore this program prints *Phew!*.**
- ☐ Since we removed "rats" from the animals list, the condition is False. Nothing is printed to the console.
- ☐ Since we removed "mice" from the animals list, the condition is True. Therefore this program prints *Call the rat catcher!*.
- ☐ Since we removed "cats" from the animals list, the condition is False. Therefore this program prints *Call the rat catcher!*.

DICTIONARIES AND DICTIONARY FUNCTIONS

Q: What is true of dictionaries?
- ☐ **You can fit multiple key-value pairs in a single dictionary, separating them with commas.**
- ☐ You can fit multiple key-value pairs in a multiple dictionaries, separating them with semicolon.
- ☐ You can fit one key-value pair per dictionary.
- ☐ You can fit multiple key-value pairs in a single dictionary, separating them with identation.

Q: Which of the following statements about a dictionary in Python are true?
- ☐ **A dictionary is a built-in type of object in Python.**
- ☐ A dictionary has a limited number of entries.
- ☐ A dictionary can be used to store methods.
- ☐ A dictionary always needs to be imported first.

Q: How can you access a value in a dictionary?
- ☐ You can access it using its value.
- ☐ **You can access it using its key.**
- ☐ You can access it using its pair.
- ☐ You can access it using its function.

Q: In the following example, what needs to be inserted in X to have Python print the value "Go"?
goal = {"Let": "Go"}
habit = goal[X]
print(habit)

☐ X needs to be "2".
☐ X needs ti be "habit".
☐ **X needs to be "Let".**
☐ X needs to be "Go".

Q: Knowing you can also overwrite existing values in a dictionary, what is the output of the following code?
goal = {"Let": "Go"}
goal ["Let"] = "Do"
print(goal)

☐ {'Let': 'Let'}
☐ {'Do': 'Let'}
☐ {'Let': 'Go'}
☐ **{'Do': 'Go'}**

Q: When you compare lists and dictionaries, what is one of the main differences between these two?

☐ Dictionaries hold values while lists do not.
☐ Lists hold values while dictionaries do not.
☐ Lists use keys while dictionaries use indexes.
☐ **Dictionaries use keys while lists use indexes.**

Q: What is the output of the following program?
seven = {'one': 1, 'two': 2, 'three': 3, 'four': 4}
print(seven['two']

☐ 3
☐ **2**
☐ 1
☐ four

Q: What is the output of the following program?
seven = {'one': 1, 'two': 2, 'three': 3, 'four': 4}
print(seven['two']

☐ 3
☐ **2**
☐ 1
☐ four

Q: What is the function with which you can see all of the keys in a dictionary?
- ☐ **keys( )**
- ☐ values( )
- ☐ allkeys( )
- ☐ allvalues( )

Q: How can you print all the keys in the dictionary "names"?
- ☐ **names.keys( )**
- ☐ names.keys
- ☐ keys(names)
- ☐ keys( ).names

Q: How can you check if a dictionary contains a certain key?
- ☐ contain
- ☐ out
- ☐ **in**
- ☐ from

Q: Also, how can you update multiple values at once?
- ☐ overwrite( )
- ☐ **update( )**
- ☐ reinsert( )
- ☐ refresh( )

Q: You need to remove a value from a dictionary. How do you do this?
- ☐ By using the function delete( ) and specifying which key to remove.
- ☐ By using the function out( ) and specifying which key to remove.
- ☐ By using the function remove( ) and specifying which key to remove.
- ☐ **By using the function pop( ) and specifying which key to remove.**

Q: How do you delete the key-value pair with key 'Same' from a dictionary 'Songs'?
- ☐ Songs.delete('Same')
- ☐ **Songs.pop('Same')**
- ☐ remove(Songs, 'Same')
- ☐ delete(Songs, 'Same')

Q: What is the advantage of using loops?
- ☐ Loops act as brackets around similar functions.
- ☐ **Using loops, you can avoid writing the exact same line of code several times and therefore remove duplication.**
- ☐ Without loops, Python doesn't work through identical lines of code.
- ☐ Loops serve as functions within repeated statements.

Q: What is the output of the following code?
for i in range(3):
   print(i)
- ☐ **0**
  1
  2
- ☐ i
- ☐ range(3)
- ☐ 3

Q: When looking at the line "for i in n", what does i stand for?
- ☐ The loop variable i takes on the countervalues of the loop.
- ☐ The loop variable i equals to the function values before the loop.
- ☐ The loop variable i equals n.
- ☐ **The loop variable i in the loop takes on each value in whatever the loop is iterating over.**

Q: Is it mandatory to use the "i" in loops?
- ☐ No, it is not. Loop variables can be names however we like, including reservec keywords.
- ☐ **No, it is not. Loop variables can be named however we like, except for reserved keywords.**
- ☐ Yes, it is mandatory. If named otherwise, Python will not detect the loop.
- ☐ It depends on the Python version used.

Q: What is the output of this code?
breeds = ["bulldog", "terrier", "foxhound"]

for cat in breeds:
   print(cat)
- ☐ Syntax Error, since cats are not dog breeds.
- ☐ cat
- ☐ Syntax Error, since the loop variable i hasn't been used.
- ☐ **bulldog**
  terrier
  foxhound

Q: What is the output of this code?

breeds = ["bulldog", "terrier", "foxhound"]

for for in breeds:
  print(for)

- ☑ **Syntax Error: invalid syntax since for is a reserved keyword.**
- ☐ Syntax Error: invalid syntax due to duplication of the word 'for'.
  bulldog
- ☐ terrier
  foxhound
- ☐ It will print the word 'for' since it is a reserved keyword.

Q: How many times does this program print "Nice to meet you!"?

n = ["n", "b", "c"]
for i in n:
  print("Nice to meet you!")

- ☐ "Nice to meet you!" is printed two times since the index starts at 0.
- ☑ **"Nice to meet you!" is printed three times since there are three elements in the list n.**
- ☐ "Nice to meet you!" is not printed at all since it is not part of the list.
- ☐ SyntaxError: invalid syntax since n is a reserved keyword.

Q: What is the output of this program?

m = ""
for i in range(3):
  m = m + str(i)
print(m)

- ☐ i
- ☐ 123
- ☐ 3
- ☑ **012**

Q: We've looked at for loops. What is true for while loops?

- ☐ A while loop executes code only when its condition is false.
- ☐ A while loop stops when its condition is true.
- ☑ **A while loop executes code as long as its condition is true.**
- ☐ A while loop doesn't depent on conditions.

Q: How many times will the following while loop print "number"?

number = 3
while number > 0:
  print(number)
  number = number -1

- ☐ Once: -1.
- ☐ Twice: 3, 2, then stop because number = 0.
- ☐ **Three times: 3, 2, 1, then stop because number = 0.**
- ☐ Four times: 3, 2, 1, 0, then stop because number = 0.

Q: What is the keyword called used to exit out of a while loop?
- ☐ **break**
- ☐ stop
- ☐ out
- ☐ exit

Q: What does Python print to the console?

bun = 0
while True:
  if bun == 8:
    break
  else:
    bun += 1
  print(bun)

- ☐ bun
- ☐ 1, 2, 3, 4, 5, 6, 7, 8
- ☐ **8**
- ☐ False

Q: Now with the right condition, while loops can become infinite. What about this one?

z = 0
while z >= 0:
  print("Infinity")
  z += 1

- ☐ It is finite, since z only adds 1 after printing the word "Infinity".
- ☐ It cannot be finite, since there is not break keyword in the code.
- ☐ **It is infinite, since z will always be greater than 0 due to the z +=1 line.**
- ☐ It is finite, because the condition will turn out False.

ADVANCED PYTHON

TOOLS

Q: What is an easier way to add up numbers without using a for loop?
- ☐ Combining two for loops.
- ☐ **Using the sum() function.**
- ☐ Adding numbers using +=.
- ☐ There is no easier way.

Q: Which of the following statements *is true* for the sum() function?
- ☐ It can sum up integers and floats, but not complex numbers.
- ☐ It can sum up integers, floats and complex numbers, but it will always output an integer.
- ☐ It can only sum up integers.
- ☐ **It can sum up integers, floats and complex numbers.**

Q: Which function allows me to easily access a sequence of integers in Python?
- ☐ **Using the range() function will output every integer between start and stop -1.**
- ☐ Using the range() function will output every integer between start -1 and stop -1.
- ☐ Using the range() function will output every integer between start -1 and stop.
- ☐ Using the range() function will output every integer between start and stop.

Q: What happens if the range() function only contains a stop integer?
- ☐ A syntax error will appear.
- ☐ **Python will assume the range to start from 0.**
- ☐ It will only output the stop integer.
- ☐ Python will assume the range to start from 1.

Q: Chaning an existing value can be done using assignments like +=. For example, A += B is equivalent to A = A + B. What other assignments are valid?
- ☐ *=
- ☐ /=
- ☐ -=
- ☐ #=

Q: What happens when you use int() on a float?
- ☐ It rounds up or down everything after the decimal point.
- ☐ It will add a "0" after the first decimal place.
- ☐ **It just cuts off everything after the decimal point.**
- ☐ It will output a syntax error.

Q: What happens when you use round() on a float?
- ☑ **It rounds up or down everything after the decimal point.**
- ☐ It will add a "0" after the first decimal place.
- ☐ It just cuts off everything after the decimal point.
- ☐ It will output a syntax error.

Q: What is the correct way to write the range() function?
- ☑ **a = range(2, 5)**
- ☐ a : range[2, 5]
- ☐ a = range(2; 5)
- ☐ a = range[2: 5]

INDEXING

Q: What can you do by using indexing with ":"?
- ☐ Sum up ranges.
- ☑ **See ranges of strings and lists.**
- ☐ Calculating new values.
- ☐ Changing existing values.

Q: Which one of these lines will output the whole string *str = "this is not a pipe"*?
- ☐ str[all]
- ☐ str[0:17]
- ☐ str[0:2]
- ☑ **str[0:len(str)]**

Q: What happens if you leave out a value for the beginning or end of a range?
- ☐ Python will ask where you want to start / end.
- ☐ Python will output a syntax error.
- ☑ **Python will assume you want to start at the start or end of the string/list.**
- ☐ Python will assume you want to start at the start +1 and end -1 of the string/list.

Q: Given the list *four_ears = ["relationship", "self-revelation", "factual", "appeal"]*, which of these will give out the last two list elements ["factual", "appeal"]?
- ☐ four_ears[:2]
- ☑ **four_ears[2:]**
- ☐ four_ears[:]
- ☐ four_ears[0:3]

Q: Assuming we have a list of strings *four_ears = ["relationship", "self-revelation", "factual", "appeal"]*, how can we find the first letter of the third string?

- ☐ four_ears[1][3]
- ☐ four_ears[0][2]
- ☐ four_ears[3][0]
- ☐ **four_ears[2][0]**

Q: Given this line of code *hello_there = "obi wan kenobi"*, which one of the following <u>does not</u> return the whole string "obi wan kenobi"?

- ☐ **hello_there[0:len(hello_there)-1]**
- ☐ hello_there[:]
- ☐ hello_there[0:len(hello_there)]
- ☐ hello_there[0:]

Q: Given this line of code *snippets = ["we will rock", "there is no", "there you go"]*, which one of the following lines of code will output "we will rock you"?

- ☐ **first = snippets[0]**
  second = snippets[2][1]   we will rock you
  print(first + second)

- ☐ first = snippets[1]
  second = snippets[0][2]   there is no rock
  print(first + second)

- ☐ first = snippets[2]
  second = snippets[3][1]   error, list index out of range
  print(first + second)

- ☐ first = snippets[3]
  second = snippets[1][2]   error, list index out of range
  print(first + second)

FUNCTIONS

Q: How can we define our own function with the name "music"?
- ☐ def music:
- ☐ Def Music
- ☐ def: music
- ☑ **def music ( ):**

Q: You can also define a function which does nothing, for instance if you want to change it later. What is the keyword for that?
- ☐ do nothing
- ☑ **pass**
- ☐ don't
- ☐ nothing

Q: What happens if we make a variable outside a function but then try giving it a different value inside the function's identation?
- ☑ **The value of the function doesn't change.**
- ☐ Python asks which value to use.
- ☐ The value of the function changes.
- ☐ Python outputs an error.

Q: What ist the output of the following code?
nice = True
def so_great():
  nice = False
so_great()
print(nice)
- ☐ nice
- ☐ so_great
- ☐ False
- ☑ **True**

Q: Which one of these statements about functions is *not true*?
- ☐ We can store what a function returns in a variable.
- ☐ Functions perform the code indented inside them.
- ☑ **We cannot use while loops inside of functions.**
- ☐ We can write functions inside of functions.

Q: What is the output of these lines?

```
def yes_four( ):
    answer = "yes"
    for i in range(4):
        print(yes_four)
```

☐ One time the word "yes".
☐ It prints the string "yes_four".
☐ These lines output an error.
☑ **Four times the word "yes".**

Q: What is the output of the following code?

```
z = 10
def z_new( ):
    z = 20
    return z
x = z_new()
print(x == 20 and z == 10)
```

☐ 30
☐ x and z
☑ **True**
☐ z_new

ARGUMENTS

Q: Functions can take inputs which are arguments and go in the parentheses after the function name. What is the output of the following function with the argument "sports":

```
def always_time_for (sports):
    return 2 * sports
always_time_for(2)
```

- ☐ 2
- ☐ **4**
- ☐ sport sports
- ☐ 2sports

Q: It is possible to put anything into a function. However, what is the drawback when using operations that only work on specific types?
- ☐ Python won't allow for other arguments in a function.
- ☐ We cannot use any other functions.
- ☐ **We limit the arguments of our function to those types.**
- ☐ Functions become restricted to a certain number of arguments.

Q: What is a docstring?
- ☐ **It is a multi-line string which can be written inside functions in order to explain what the function does and what its arguments should be.**
- ☐ It is a string used to address documents outside of the console.
- ☐ It is a single-linge string which will help check for errors in your code before running it.
- ☐ It is a special string that allows you to find any keyword entered after the word "doc".

Q: Which symbol begins a docstring?
- ☐ //
- ☐ =!
- ☐ \\
- ☐ **"""**

Q: What is the function that helps with finding out about a specific function?
- ☐ explain()
- ☐ assist()
- ☐ **help()**
- ☐ support()

Q: What is the output of the following code?

```
def welcome(name):
   ''' Takes a string and prints a welcome message.'''
   print("Welcome, " + name)

help(welcome)
```

- ☐ Welcome, name
- ☐ **Takes a string and prints a welcome message.**
- ☐ Syntax error
- ☐ welcome(name)

Q: Instead of using a docstring, you can also prevent bad inputs to functions by...?

- ☐ ...making the function as complex as possible.
- ☐ ...letting Python tell the user what to do by giving cryptic error messages.
- ☐ **...telling the user what to do instead by using the print command, e.g. print("x must be a float!").**
- ☐ ...giving the number of first level support to the user before even running the code.

Q: What is the output of the following code when z equals "x"?

```
def particle(z):
   return z * z
```

- ☐ **Error, as we can't multiply strings.**
- ☐ z
- ☐ z^2
- ☐ zz

RECURSION

Q: How can you describe recursion?

- ☐ Recursion is using a function inside of another function.
- ☐ Recursion is a variable used to form a loop.
- ☐ Recursion is defining an argument which is continually applied.
- ☐ **Recursion is calling a function inside of itself, usually using a base case and a recursive step.**

Q: What are typical use cases for recursion?

- ☐ **Factorials (an integer multiplied by every integer less than it down to 0) and Fibonacci numbers (the first two are 1 and all the others are found by adding the numbers before them).**
- ☐ If and else statements.
- ☐ Methods and arguments.
- ☐ Dictionaries and loops.

Q: What is the output of the following code?

```
def factorial(x):
    if x == 1:          # base case
        return x
    else:               # recursive step
        return x * factorial(x-1)


factorial(3)
```

- ☐ 3
- ☐ 4
- ☐ 5
- ☐ **6**

Q: What is the output of the following lines of code?

```
def fibonacci(z):
    if z == 1 or z == 2:    # base case
        return 1
    else:                   # recursive step
        return fib(z-1) + fib(n-2)


fibonacci(4)
```

- ☐ **3**
- ☐ 4
- ☐ 5
- ☐ 6

Q: When does it make sense to use recursion?
- ☐ When we want to calculate a function inside of another function.
- ☐ **When we have to compute something similar over and over for many different inputs.**
- ☐ When we want to overwrite an existing function.
- ☐ When we are not sure how to define the arguments of a function.

CLASSES

Q: Python allows for more flexibility than just built-in types. What is the keyword used to define own objects?
- ☐ def
- ☐ own
- ☐ category
- ☐ **class**

Q: Having defined a new class, how do you tell Python to make an object of that class?
- ☐ **Using the function __init__().**
- ☐ Using the function __init__:
- ☐ Using the function _init_()
- ☐ Using the function init:

Q: Classes can have attributes. But what are attributes?
- ☐ Attributes are functions used to overwrite existing arguments.
- ☐ **Attributes are stored properties which can be accessed and changed.**
- ☐ Attributes allow for indexes to be drawn upon.
- ☐ Attributes are the last part of if and else statements.

Q: How can you access existing attributes defined in the class definition?
- ☐ **By using a . after the object's name.**
- ☐ By using the function *get*.
- ☐ By printing the attribute.
- ☐ By calling the right index within the class.

Q: What is the output of the following code?
class Sunny:
  a = 5
  b = 10
  def __init__(self):
    pass
z = Point()
print(z.a)
z.a = 1
print(z.b)

☐ a
  b
☐ Error message for not using the *get* function to call on the attributes a and b.
☐ **5**
  10
☐ Point.5

Q: Setting attributes is also possible by making them arguments to the __init__()
function. What is the benefit of doing this though?
☐ This way, they can be called upon more easily by using the *get* function.
☐ The __init__() function sets these attributes as a default throughout the code.
☐ The use of the __init__() function operates as a trigger to those arguments.
☐ **This way, you can set them at the same time when creating a new object.**

Q: What is the output of the following code?
class Song:
  def __init__(self, title, artist):
  self.title = title
  self.artist = artist

play = Song("Imagine", "John Lennon")
print(play.title)
☐ **"Imagine"**
☐ "John Lennon"
☐ "Song"
☐ "Title"

Q: In Python, what is a method?
☐ A method is a means to print to the console.
☐ A method is a statements inside of a function.
☐ **A method is a function inside of a class.**
☐ A method is an argument inside of an else statement

Q: What has to be the first argument for any method?
- ☐ this
- ☐ that
- ☐ mine
- ☑ **self**

Q: What is the correct way to call on a method?
- ☑ **Using a . after the object's name.**
- ☐ Using a " before the object's name.
- ☐ Using a m after the object's name.
- ☐ Using a * before the object's name.

INHERITANCE

Q: How can you describe inheritance?
- ☐ When closing a class, its attributes are given to the next class in the code.
- ☑ **When having multiple classes that have attributes in common, we can build a general class and then make more specific derived classes.**
- ☐ When looking at three classes, one class will receive particular characteristics from the other two.
- ☐ When having a class that impacts other classes in close proximity to it.

Q: Looking at the following code, which one is the base class and which ones are the more specific classes?

```
class Animals:
    def __init__(self, type, name):
        self.type = type
        self.name = name

    def change_type(self, type):
        self.type = type

    def change_name(self, name):
        self.name = name
```

- ☐ The first two classes are the base classes and the last one is the more speific class.
- ☐ The second class ("change_type") is the base class and the other two are the more specific classes.
- ☐ The last class ("change_name") is the base class and the other two are the more specific classes.
- ☑ **The first class ("__init__") is the base class and the following two are the more specific classes.**

Q: How can we make a derived class?
- ☐ Put the name of the derived class in brackets.
- ☐ **Put the name of the base class in parentheses.**
- ☐ Put the name of the base class behind the derived class separated by a dot.
- ☐ Put the name of the derived class behind the base class separated by a dot.

Q: What is the output of the following code?
class Parent(Family):
  pass

dad = Parent("Jack", 42)
dad.change_age(43)
print(dad.age)
- ☐ 42
- ☐ "Jack"
- ☐ **43**
- ☐ "Parent"

Q: Having defined an initializer, what about adding more attributes and methods to derived classes?
- ☐ **More attributes and methods can be added to derived classes to store specific things where they are different from other dervied classes.**
- ☐ You can only add one attribute or method at a time and it has to be in a specific order.
- ☐ Once a class has been initialized, there is no adding of additional attributes and methods afterwards.
- ☐ Classes do not contain attributes and methods.

Q: Which one of the following statements is not true?
- ☐ There can be as many levels of base and derviced classes as wanted.
- ☐ The derived classes inherit all the methods of its base class.
- ☐ With inheritance, we can make related classes without having to repeat code.
- ☐ **We cannot add any additional attributes to derived classes.**

MODULES

Q: What are modules?
- [ ] Modules are objects which have unique attributes and behavior.
- [ ] **Modules are libraries of functions, values and classes which can be used in individual programs.**
- [ ] Modules are self-contained units within lines of code.
- [ ] Modules are chunks of IT architecture code is built around.

Q: The module math is a very useful one, for example when calculating the square root of a variable. However, we don't want to repeat syntax. How can be bypass having to use the math.sqrt() function repeatedly?
- [ ] We can write a class where the function is renamed to a shorter name.
- [ ] We can write a function wich repeats the line of codes for how often needed.
- [ ] We can use recursion on importing modules.
- [ ] **We can use the keyword "as" so we can refer to the module using a shorter name.**

Q: What is the output of the following code?
import math as m
m.sqrt(16)
- [ ] **4**
- [ ] 2
- [ ] 8
- [ ] 10

Q: Knowing you only need a few functions from a module, how could you import just these few functions and avoid the "." syntax altogether?
- [ ] By using the keyword in, e.g. *in math import cos*
- [ ] By using the keyword out, e.g. *out math import cos*
- [ ] **By using the keyword from, e.g. *from math import cos***
- [ ] By using the keyword of, e.g. *of math import cos*

Q: If you're not sure what functions from a module are needed and you would like to import everything within a module, how can you do this?
- [ ] **By using *, e.g. *from math import ***
- [ ] By using the keyword all, e.g. *from math import all*
- [ ] By using (), e.g. *from math import ()*
- [ ] By using the keyword complete, e.g. *complete import from math*

Q: How can you access information on specific module functions?
- ☐ The print(help) function gives information on what's printed to the console.
- ☐ **The help() function will give information on any imported functions.**
- ☐ Read the documentation or ask first level support.
- ☐ Information is automatically given when importing the module functions.

Q: How can you import multiple modules?
- ☐ **By listing them separated by a comma, e.g. *import math, random*.**
- ☐ By listing them separated by a semicolon, e.g. *import math; random*.
- ☐ By writing them inside of parentheses, e.g. *import(math, random)*.

  The only way to import multiple modules is by importing them separately, e.g.
- ☐ *import math*

  import random

Q: What does the module random do?
- ☐ It has functions for doing random unit tests.
- ☐ It has functions for randomly debugging code.
- ☐ It has functions for generating random arguments in classes.
- ☐ **It has functions for choosing numbers randomly.**

Q: What is the output of the following code?

import math, random
 # pick a number between 1 and 20
number = random.randint(1, 20)
math.sqrt(number)
- ☐ The square root of the number chosen by the user.
- ☐ Syntax error.
- ☐ **The square root of the randomly picked number between 1 and 20.**
- ☐ 5

Q: What does the module datetime do?
- ☐ It calculates time zones for different countries.
- ☐ It gives back the current date and time.
- ☐ It contains the calendar of the last five years.
- ☐ **It contains functions for working with times and dates.**

Q: What is the output of the following lines of code?

import random
def throw_dices():
  dice_one = random.randint(1,6)
  dice_two = random.randint(1,6)
  return dice_one + dice_two
- ☐ This code will return the first dice roll.
- ☐ This code will return first one, then the other dice roll.
- ☐ **This code will return the sum of two dice rolls.**
- ☐ This code will return the second dice roll.

Q: Which of the following import statements is not valid?
a) import math
*b) from math import **
c) import sin from math
d) import math as m

- [ ] a
- [ ] b
- [ ] **c**
- [ ] d

Q: What does this function do?
*from dateime import **
def day_until 2022(day):
  countdown = date(2022, 1, 1)
  time = countdown – day
  return time.days

- [ ] This function returns the years until 2022.
- [ ] This function subtracts the days passed.
- [ ] This function calculates the age I will be on January 1, 2022.
- [ ] **This function counts down to January 1, 2022.**

RECOMMENDATIONS

Want to learn more about coding with Python? Here are some recommended books on python to further your skills:

- "Automating the boring stuff with Python" by Al Sweigart
- "Python Crash Course" by Eric Matthes
- "Fluent Python" by Luciano Ramalho
- "Dive into Python" by Mark Pilgrim
- "Python Cookbook" by Brian K. Jones and David M. Beazly

Also, a great tip is to start doing a lot of small, beginner-friendly projects, for example:

- Tic-Tac-Toe
- Calculator
- Alarm Clock
- Calendar
- PacMan
- Password Generator
- Rock, Paper, Scissors Game.

Last but not least, code-alongs are a great way to get into the programming logic and learn how established coders approach new projects. I personally recommend the channel "the Come Up" by Bukola and her "code with me" videos. Enjoy!